YORKSHIRE DALES
Loving it!

IAN McVETY

HALSGROVE

DEDICATION

This book is dedicated to those that have inspired it and to those that it may inspire.

First published in Great Britain in 2011

British Library Cataloguing-in-Publication Data
A CIP record for this title is available from the
British Library

ISBN 978 0 85704 023 7

HALSGROVE
Halsgrove House,
Ryelands Business Park,
Bagley Road, Wellington,
Somerset TA21 9PZ
Tel: 01823 653777
Fax: 01823 216796
email: sales@halsgrove.com

Part of the Halsgrove group of companies.
Information on all Halsgrove titles is
available at: www.halsgrove.com

Printed and bound in China by
Everbest Printing Co Ltd

INTRODUCTION

The Yorkshire Dales sit astride the central Pennines covering an area of 1762 square kilometres or 680 square miles. The nearest urban conurbations are Manchester 50 miles to the south west and Bradford and Leeds to the south east. The principal towns of the Dales are Skipton, Settle, Ilkley and Harrogate.

The term "dale", referring to a valley, originates from Old Norse and in very many of the place names throughout these valleys are references to the people who settled them so many years ago. The southerly dales tend to follow a north to south direction, such as Ribblesdale and Wharfedale, whilst the more northerly dales tend to run east to west, for example Swaledale and Wensleydale.

Perhaps my favourite dale is Swaledale, particularly in winter time when the isolation of the upper valley is obvious, often being cut off in times of snow. Birkdale Common sits high above the dale, with its acidic heather moorland atop the coarse gritstone. The River Swale carves through geological time as the valley reaches Keld, then Thwaite and Muker and all the while it plunges over waterfalls with magnificent carboniferous limestone steps, so characteristic of these parts.

This book wends its way over fells, down valleys and over drover's tracks, which marked the ancient routes used for millennia to connect one dale to the other. Viewing these images it is not hard to see how Man has contributed to the scenery, with his clearings and walls helping to create and define this most glorious of landscapes.

Cleasby Hill at the northern end of the Yorkshire Dales sits high above Arkengarthdale.

Fremmington Edge overlooks the River Arkle which winds its way down the valley to join the River Swale at the popular market town of Reeth.

Whernside. Higher than its namesake Great Whernside, it is the highest of the Three Peaks, though by no means as distinctive in profile as its two brothers.

Faggergill Moor was once a hive of industry with mining providing a bleak and remote existence for the workers.

Gregareth. This is where Lancashire bounds Yorkshire and where the watershed provides acidic rainwater to Ease Gill so that it may cut through the overlying gritstone in to the carboniferous limestone where it forms England's longest and most complex cave system.

High above Chapel le Dale this spectacular limestone erratic on Scales Moor looks on towards Ingleborough.

Ingleborough sits regally above Chapel le Dale. The second highest of the Three Peaks, its summit bears traces of what was thought to be a hill fort, though recent studies point more towards the remains being of symbolic significance.

Ingleborough in winter. Cold moist air swirls through the valley below.

Some winter sunshine is welcome relief to the hardy sheep of the North Yorkshire fells.

Blea Moor, where the Settle to Carlisle railway traverses the Ribblehead Viaduct. This remote spot was for several years home for the hardy men who built this feat of engineering, living in temporary villages such as Sebastopol, Belgravia, Jericho and Jerusalem in the remote and desolate landscape.

Thorns. This now abandoned hamlet was once an important resting place on the pack horse trail. Nan Bottom Lane ran through this former monastic lodge for Furness Abbey. Now little remains except traces of buildings and a barn.

Whernside from Southerscales in late summer. The grykes in between the limestone clints provide shelter from where grow ferns and the occasional tree.

Gritstone erratics at Norber above Clapham are a source of geological wonderment. This one is perched on three small limestone pedestals, the remainder of its base having been washed away in solution.

Moughton Scar lies at the head of Crummack Dale and bounds the edge of one of the country's largest areas of limestone pavement.

Abandoned Farmhouse. Hunterstye Lane, the ancient pack-horse road on which it lies, eventually wends its way to Beecroft Hall in Ribblesdale.

Halton Gill is a tiny hamlet near the head of the beautiful and remote valley of Littondale. Here it is caught in evening light during spring as storm clouds gather above.

Heather moorland above Littondale in early autumn.

Pen-y-Ghent. As seen over the limestone pavement at Moughton.

Snow sculpted by dry easterly winds settles amongst the limestone pavements in winter time.

Pen-y-Ghent Gill flows through a deep ravine which cuts through a landscape of ancient settlements.

Brimham Rocks high above Nidderdale are a myriad of tors that nestle atop one another poised precariously. A source of delight for climbers with such names as The Druid's Writing Desk, Dancing Bear, The Turtle and Indian's Turban it does not take much imagination to see how they got their names.

Littondale bathed in summer sunshine. These lush green fields ripen below Plover Hill in a scene typical of the Yorkshire Dales.

Malham Tarn with Great Close Scar in evening sunshine.

Bleaberry Pots above the Walden valley, a small tributary off Bishopdale.

Semer Water sits quietly in the tiny valley of Raydale, a subsidiary of Wensleydale.

Evening grazing Hardy sheep graze on the fells as the sun goes down behind Ingleborough.

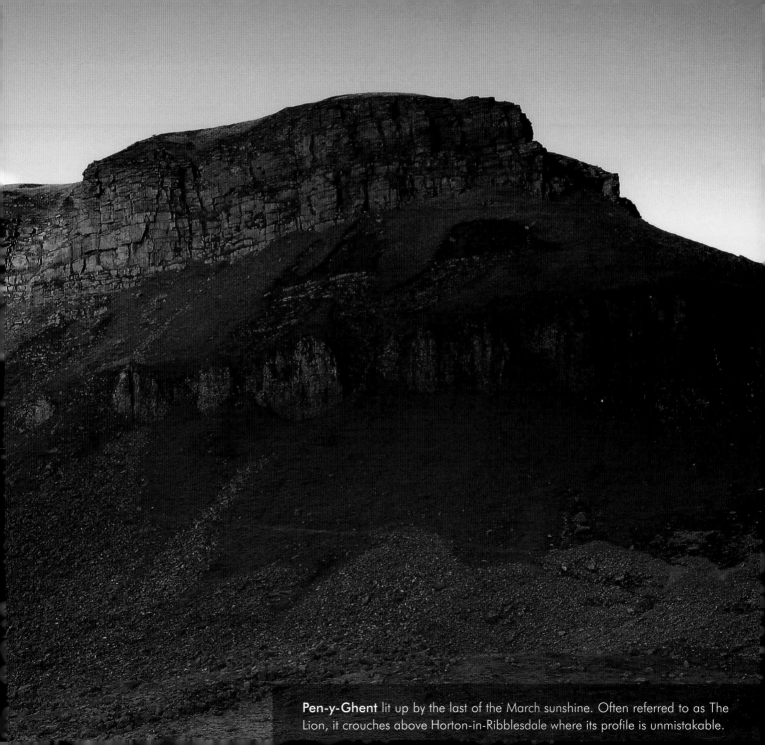

Pen-y-Ghent lit up by the last of the March sunshine. Often referred to as The Lion, it crouches above Horton-in-Ribblesdale where its profile is unmistakable.

A cairn marks who knows what?

Stainforth Force. One of the characteristics of the Dales is the waterfalls that cascade through the valleys. Here the River Ribble crashes through the valley.

The traces of long forgotten industry can be seen all around the Dales. Stonesdale near Swaledale is no exception where the landscape is dotted with mines.

Field barn in Swaledale.

Birkdale Tarn lies high on the peaty soil of the northern edge of the Yorkshire Dales.

Farming can be difficult in the best of times, but when the fields are covered in snow the upper reaches of the valleys can be virtually inaccessible.

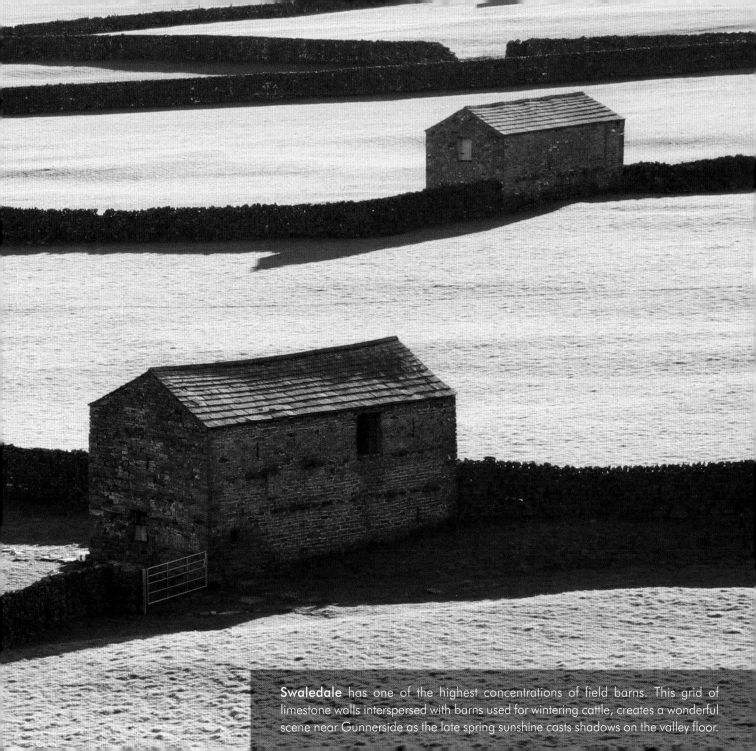

Swaledale has one of the highest concentrations of field barns. This grid of limestone walls interspersed with barns used for wintering cattle, creates a wonderful scene near Gunnerside as the late spring sunshine casts shadows on the valley floor.

Great Shunner Fell draped in snow on a clear, crisp winter's day.

Greets Shooting House above Wensleydale with its built-in fireplace would have once provided refuge for shooting parties high on the grouse moorland.

Gunnerside was the centre of European lead production in the nineteenth century. All that is left is the lunar landscape of crushed stone and the network of tracks shown by the melting snow.

Upper Swaledale in winter.

Oxnup Scar closes in on the tiny road connecting Swaledale to Wensleydale.

Wain Wath Force on the River Swale in autumn. The leaves turn golden and the warm afternoon sun bathes the limestone steps.

Addelborough overlooks Wensleydale in winter.

Aysgarth Falls, Wensleydale where the River Ure descends through the limestone strata in three distinct steps. Painted by Turner and visited by Ruskin and Wordsworth, this beautiful scene has been a popular tourist destination for over 200 years.

Cam High Road climbs from the ancient Roman town of Bainbridge in Wensleydale, with Green Scar, Addelborough and Heights of Hazely in the distance. This once Roman road climbs to 586 metres before descending towards Ribblehead. It later became a popular route for drovers moving cattle to market.

Hill farming on Yorburgh above Wensleydale.

The upper reaches of Gordale Beck cross the Mastiles Lane near the site of a Roman fort.

Bluebell woods.

Welcome sunshine breaks through the cloud above Wensleydale after a deluge of rain has soaked the valley below.

Cracoe War Memorial.

Crookrise. Outcrops of millstone grit project out over Embsay on the southern edges of the Dales.

The fells above Hetton, Wharfedale.

The Strid. In a traditional feat of skill and bravery the foolhardy would run across the adjacent rocks and leap across the gushing torrent of the River Wharfe. Legend would have us believe that a young noble boy named Romiley was returning from hunting on Barden Moor one evening when he attempted to cross The Strid. His greyhound, which he was leading, faltered and Romiley drowned in the Wharfe. His grieving parents Alicia and William FitzDuncan bequeathed the land to the monks of Embsay where Bolton Abbey now stands.

Great Whernside. This wind-sculpted gritstone summit with its broad ridged flanks was the scene of several flying tragedies in the Second World War, as pilots returning to the nearby airfields in the Vale of York tragically failed to navigate this large elevated obstacle.

Late afternoon sunshine paints the snow.

Widdale. A small enclosed coppice looking towards Hawes.

Gritstone erratics at Norber.